BENJAMIN FRANKLIN

A Photo-Illustrated Biography
by T.M. Usel

Historical Consultant
Steve Potts
Professor of History

Bridgestone Books

an Imprint of Capstone Press

Facts about Benjamin Franklin

- Ben Franklin helped write both the Declaration of Independence and the Constitution.
- He invented the Franklin stove. It was used to heat buildings throughout North America and Europe. He also invented the lightning rod and bifocal glasses.
- He conducted a famous kite experiment to prove that lightning is electricity.
- He signed the treaty that ended the Revolutionary War.

Bridgestone Books are published by Capstone Press • 818 North Willow Street, Mankato, Minnesota 56001
Copyright © 1996 by Capstone Press • All rights reserved • Printed in the United States of America

Library of Congress Cataloging-in-Publication Data
Usel, T.M.
　　Benjamin Franklin, a photo-illustrated biography/T.M. Usel.
　　p. cm.
　　Includes bibliographical references and index.
　　ISBN 1-56065-342-6
　　1. Franklin, Benjamin, 1706-1790--Juvenile literature. 2. Franklin, Benjamin, 1706-1790--Pictorial works--Juvenile literature. 3.Statesmen--United States--Biography--Juvenile literature. 4. Statesmen--United States--Pictorial works--Juvenile literature. 5. Inventors--United States--Biography--Juvenile literature. 6. Inventors--United States--Pictorial works--Juvenile literature.7. Printers--United States--Biography--Juvenile literature.8. Printers--United States--Pictorial works--Juvenile literature. 9.Scientists--United States--Biography--Juvenile literature. 10. Scientists--United States--Pictorial works--Juvenile literature. I. Title.
E302.6.F8U6 1996
973.3'092--dc20
[B]
95-46665
CIP
AC

Photo credits
Archive Photos: cover, 6, 10, 12, 20
Corbis-Be...

Table of Contents

Words in **boldface** type in the text are defined in the Words to Know section in the back of this book.

A Simple Craftsman

Benjamin Franklin is best known for helping build the United States of America.

But Ben was also an **inventor**, a printer, a publisher, and a writer. And he was a scientist and a **diplomat.**

Ben Franklin lived from 1706 to 1790. He spent most of his life in Philadelphia. It was the largest city in the **colony** of Pennsylvania.

The colonies offered many opportunities. Ben Franklin was smart. And he was very successful.

Ben Franklin accomplished his goals through his own hard work. He was born into a poor family. He died a rich man. He had little schooling. But Ben was admired by many people for his knowledge.

We remember Ben Franklin for his role in shaping the United States of America. But Ben liked to think of himself as a printer. He considered himself a simple craftsman.

Ben Franklin thought of himself as a simple craftsman.

The Early Years

Benjamin Franklin was born on January 17, 1706, in Boston, in the colony of Massachusetts. His parents were Josiah and Abiah Franklin. Ben was the 15th of 17 children.

Ben went to school for only two years. He studied Latin, reading, writing, and arithmetic. Ben loved books and could not stop reading. Ben was 10 years old when he finished school. It was time to learn to make soap and candles as his father did.

Tradespeople often worked 12 to 14 hours a day. Ben did not mind the long hours, but he hated the work. He wanted to be a sailor.

Ben's father was afraid Ben would run away to become a sailor. Ben's older brother had already died at sea. Josiah tried to find Ben a job on land.

Ben agreed to become an **apprentice,** or student worker, for his brother James. Ben would learn to be a printer.

When he was young, Ben often worked 12 to 14 hours a day.

Reader and Writer

In the 1700s, many people could not read. The Bible was the only book owned by most families. Ben was different. He worked long days at the print shop, but he always found time to read.

At night, Ben would secretly borrow new books from a friend who worked in a bookstore. Ben returned the books early in the morning. The owner never knew they had been borrowed.

In 1721, Ben's brother James began his own newspaper, the *New England Courant*. It had stories about the people of Boston and New England.

One day James found a letter slipped under the door. The letter was a funny one signed by Mrs. Silence Dogood. James printed it. Readers liked it. More of Mrs. Dogood's letters mysteriously appeared in his shop. James printed them all. Mrs. Silence Dogood was actually Ben. At age 16, Ben became a published writer.

Ben worked as an apprentice in his brother's print shop.

At Home in Philadelphia

Ben enjoyed the printing business, but he did not like working for his brother James. When Ben was 17 years old, he ran away to Philadelphia.

Ben arrived in Philadelphia early one morning. He was tired and hungry. He found a bakery and ordered three pennies' worth of bread.

Ben discovered that prices were lower than in Boston. He walked out with three large rolls. His pockets were already full. They were stuffed with socks and shirts. So he carried a roll under each arm while he ate the third. Ben caught the eye of many people, including Deborah Read, who would later become his wife.

Ben liked Philadelphia. He got a job as a printer. In 1730, Ben and Deborah were married. Although they were often apart, they cared for each other very much. Ben wrote many letters to "my dear Debby."

Ben Franklin liked the city of Philadelphia.

Poor Richard, 1733.

AN
Almanack

For the Year of Chrift

1733,

Being the Firft after LEAP YEAR.

And makes fince the Creation	Years
By the Account of the Eaftern *Greeks*	7241
By the Latin Church, when ☉ ent. ♈	6932
By the Computation of *W.W.*	5742
By the *Roman* Chronology	5682
By the *Jewifh* Rabbies.	5494

Wherein is contained.

Poor Richard

When he was 22 years old, Ben Franklin opened a print shop. Deborah often helped her husband there.

Ben printed the *Pennsylvania Gazette*. The newspaper ran stories about the people of the colony. Ben wrote articles on how he felt about things. The *Gazette* was very successful.

Ben also wrote *Poor Richard's Almanack*. It contained all sorts of facts, weather forecasts, and sayings. Except for the Bible, it was the best-selling book in the colonies.

People still remember many of the sayings. Here are a few:

A penny saved is a penny earned.

Fish and visitors stink in three days.

Half the truth is often a great lie.

Early to bed and early to rise, makes a man healthy, wealthy, and wise.

Ben Franklin wrote the fact-filled *Poor Richard's Almanack*.

Scientist and Inventor

Ben Franklin made a lot of money as a printer and writer. He retired from his job when he was only 42. He then turned his attention to science.

Ben liked to figure out how and why things worked. He liked to solve problems.

Ben invented the Pennsylvania fireplace, which most people called the Franklin stove. It spreads fireplace heat evenly. Ben also created **bifocal eyeglasses** and invented the **lightning** rod.

Ben was interested in the new science of electricity. His most famous experiment used a kite and a key. He wanted to prove that lightning is electricity. To prove it, Ben and his son William flew a kite in a storm.

Lightning struck a metal rod on the kite. Ben touched a key fastened to the kite's string. There was an electrical spark. A stronger spark could have killed Ben. But he lived to tell about his discovery.

Ben used a kite and a key in his most famous experiment.

Plan to Band Together

One of Ben's ideas became the basis of the future United States of America. His plan to band the 13 colonies together came from the Iroquois Indians. Six Indian nations had joined together. Each nation was independent. Each had its own laws. In wartime, the nations joined together to fight.

The English king and the colonial assemblies turned down Ben's plan. But the idea stayed with Ben.

In 1765, many colonists were angry about the Stamp Act. England forced the colonists to buy tax stamps to put on newspapers and other items.

The colonists wanted a say in the laws that were passed. Some said Ben backed the new tax. He did not. But he had not done much to stop it.

In 1766, however, Ben stood before British officials in England. For hours he answered questions about why the colonists were so angry. The British finally withdrew the law.

Ben helped convince the British to withdraw the Stamp Act.

A New Nation

Ben spent many years in England. He tried to keep the peace between the king and the colonists. But it was no use.

While Ben sailed for home in 1775, the colonists and the British began fighting the Revolutionary War. The colonies had accepted the idea of banding together under one government.

Ben helped write the Declaration of Independence. In this document, the 13 American colonies declared their independence from England. The famous document was adopted on July 4, 1776.

During the Revolutionary War, Ben secretly sailed to France. If the British had found him, they would have hanged him as a traitor.

Ben asked the French to send troops and supplies to the colonists. The French were a big help. The fighting finally ended in 1781. The Americans won the war and their independence.

Ben Franklin helped write the Declaration of Independence.

The Final Years

Ben had a daughter, Sally, and two sons, Francis and William. Little Franky died of smallpox when he was four years old. Ben never got over being sad.

William also caused his father to be sad. William was royal governor of New Jersey during the Revolutionary War. He remained loyal to the king of England. William was jailed during the war.

Ben was almost 80 years old when he returned home from France. He had worked hard for the United States. In 1787, he attended the constitutional convention where many of his ideas were used in planning the new government. It was his idea to have a Congress with two parts, the House and the Senate.

Ben died of **pleurisy** on April 17, 1790. He was 84 years old. Ben had lived long enough to see the birth of a new nation, the United States of America.

Ben lived long enough to see the birth of the United States.

Words from Ben Franklin

"We must indeed all hang together. Or most assuredly we shall all hang separately."

After signing the Declaration of Independence, which was adopted on July 4, 1776.

"May we never have another war. For in my opinion there never was a good war or a bad peace."

After signing the peace treaty between the United States and England in 1783.

Important Dates in Ben Franklin's Life

1706 – Born in Boston, Massachusetts

1718 – Becomes a printer's apprentice

1723 – Runs away to Philadelphia

1728 – Opens a print shop in Philadelphia

1730 – Marries Deborah Read

1732 – First issue of *Poor Richard's Almanack*

1752 – Conducts kite experiment

1754 – Writes plan of union for the colonies

1774 – Deborah dies

1776 – Signs Declaration of Independence

1783 – Signs Treaty of Paris ending Revolutionary War

1787 – Attends Constitutional Convention

1790 – Dies of pleurisy at his home in Philadelphia

Words to Know

apprentice—person who works for another without pay or for low pay in return for learning a trade

bifocal eyeglasses—glasses that correct near and distant vision

colony—group of people who settle in a distant land but remain under control of their native country. The 13 British colonies in North America became the original United States.

diplomat—person appointed to represent his government in its dealings with other governments

inventor—person who thinks up and makes something that did not exist before

lightning—large, high-voltage electrical discharge that occurs in the atmosphere

pleurisy—inflammation of the tissue that covers the lungs and lines the chest cavity

Read More

Adler, David. *Benjamin Franklin: Printer, Inventor, Statesman.* New York: Holiday House, 1992.

Graves, Charles P. *Benjamin Franklin: Man of Ideas.* New York: Chelsea House, 1993.

Quackenbush, Robert. *Benjamin Franklin and His Friends.* New York: Pippin Press, 1991.

Scarf, Maggi. *Meet Benjamin Franklin.* New York: Random House, 1989.

Useful Addresses

Franklin Institute Science Museum
Benjamin Franklin National Memorial
20th Street and Benjamin Franklin Parkway
Philadelphia, PA 19103

National Archives
Pennsylvania Avenue and Eighth Street NW
Washington, DC 20408

Independence National Historical Park
313 Walnut Street
Philadelphia, PA 19106

National Museum of American History
14th Street and Constitution Avenue NW
Washington, DC 20560

Index